AF326930

Dedication

This book is dedicated to all woods wanderers, to those who know the land's friendship and draw strength from the rhythms of the earth.

Rural Route Reflections

by Kathleen S. Abrams

Entwood Publishing, Wausau, Wisconsin

Rural Route Reflections
Copyright © by Kathleen S. Abrams
All Rights Reserved
Printed in the United States of America
First Edition
ISBN: 0-9605978-0-8

Library of Congress Catalog Number: 81-66908

Illustrations by Oberon Leslie

Entwood Publishing
P.O. Box 268
Wausau, Wis. 54401

Acknowledgements

Many people helped make this book possible. My special thanks to:

Mike Jacobi, editor of Fox River Patriot, who first showed an interest in my reflections. Many of the stories in this collection were printed first in Fox River Patriot.

Oberon Leslie whose quality drawings illustrate these reflections and whose enthusiasm for my publishing ventures is always welcome.

And to Larry who encouraged this project from the beginning. His expert skills as proofreader and general consultant were much appreciated. But it is his companionship as a fellow woods wanderer I cherish most.

Table of Contents

Country Places

My address never fits on forms. The last few letters tilt off the edge, are scribbled in the margin or eliminated altogether for want of little squares to hold them.

As a high school senior struggling with stacks of application blanks, I complained to my mother. "I wish our address was shorter," I said.

"I'd rather live on Chippewa River Drive in the country," she answered, "than 1st Ave. in town. The name's more interesting."

When I moved away from Chippewa River Drive, I avoided 1st Street and 37th Ave. and decided on Trappe River Road. I just couldn't seem to settle for less.

The names of country roads are interesting. They hint at the dreams and weaknesses of the people who first felt the awesome responsiblity of naming them.

In summer, I like to turn onto Green Valley Road and pretend that I am a hot and dusty pioneer seeing this lush valley for the first time. It looks even more beautiful to me then. The little stream cutting through the valley floor sparkles with added brilliance. Scanning the divide from my vantage point atop the hill, I vow never to take my presence here lightly.

At the other end of the township is a flat, gravel road bordered by prosperous fields and impressive farm buildings. In the edge of one of these fields is a one-room schoolhouse. The once-scythed yard has grown to weeds and the bell has disappeared, but the fading-red of the painted planks still seems to shine in the afternoon sun. The road it faces is called School Road. Driving down this road, I sense the pride of the first settlers whose prosperous farms gave rise to something they valued more than money. Public education was so important to them that they named their road after the unpretentious building all but hidden beside the towering corn. School Road helps me remember this country's priorities.

In winter, I am drawn to Sugar Bush Hill Road. The snow has drifted shoulder-high against the hillside and the trees glisten bare-limbed in the frosty air. But the name on the rusting road sign reminds me that spring is coming. Soon sweet tasting sap will flow from these barren trees and campfires will cook it to a flavorful syrup. A glance at the sign assures me that I will survive the last few weeks of winter. Someone anticipated my need when he named this road Sugar Bush Hill instead of Maple Street.

The reasons for particular names are not as easy to unravel, but they inspire fascinating stories. Rocky Run is smooth blacktop now, but the name recalls days when buckboards and black buggies bounced over protruding boulders.

The Petersons have moved from Peterson Hill, but the name remains to tell of a time when hope and pride ran strong in the people who homesteaded here.

My favorite is Whiskey Road. There is a church on Whiskey Road. It finds its place between the quiet country store and an abandoned farm. These buildings help to keep the secret of Whiskey Road. They offer no clues as to the meaning of the name. Did someone christen the road in jest? Was it once a brawling, frontier street? Did a whiskey still lurk in a forgotten rock pile behind the general store?

Several years ago the bullet-riddled road sign which identified Whiskey Road disappeared. A shiny new sign renaming the road Granite Road replaced it. I suppose when city people started moving into our township, the town board decided that Whiskey Road was un-dignified. Granite Road is a solid name and reminds us of one of the township's important industries, the granite quarry. But the narrow, winding road still looks like Whiskey Road to me-- even when it meanders past the church.

In the city, street names are predictable. The streets are on one side of the river. The avenues are on the other side. All the roads running north and south are named for presidents according to their term. All the roads running east and west bear the names of trees.

In the country, the names are haphazard and varied. You have to understand the code of country names or you risk getting lost. In the city, a road with no exit is marked Dead End. In the country, we call these roads lanes. I always think that it is sad to label anything a dead end. No one wants to explore it then. But walking down a lane is romantic and exciting. I hesitate to venture down a dead end road, but I look for lanes to explore arm in arm with a favorite friend. An unexpected building, a rare flower, a quiet peace all wait for me on country lanes. Equal enchantments are probably waiting on dead end roads, but I will never find them.

Many fascinations lure country visitors. But place names have a special appeal. For some reason the sun rises more brightly on Sunrise Road. It sets with grander flare on Sunset Road. An apple scavenged from Orchard Lane tastes delicious and Deer Trail Road guarantees adventure. I feel safe on Mechanics Ridge Road because I know if my car stalls an independent fix-it man who lives just around the bend will rescue me. I like exploring country roads, but the greatest thrill of all is imagining the significance behind their colorful names.

Reflections on Land Ownership

Recently my husband and I purchased 80 acres of woodland. A simple statement, legally correct; but one which fails to convey the impact of our experience or intent of our action. Now, as I sit holding the abstract to our property, I remember the first time we saw this land. Chafing from the restraints of living in town we moved to a rural area which offered unlimited opportunity for exploration. Almost frantically we hiked, biked, picked berries and exclaimed over the numerous plants and animals with which we shared the land. Our first visitor was a half-grown procupine that ambled down our long driveway, climbed the front step and, nonchalantly raising himself to his full height, peered through the glass of our front door. In this way we met him face to face and were amused by the curiosity of our new neighbor. We were less amused by the skunk that tormented our city bred dog or the flicker that drilled a hole in our rough cedar siding, but the experiences of country living continued to be an adventure we eagerly accepted.

Often we hiked up a gravel road near our home. This road held particular fascination for us. About two miles long, it was bordered on both sides by unbroken wilderness. There were no buildings in the area and no highlines; although a portion of it was fenced, none was posted. In our experience, the road was a phenomenon.

One day we wandered farther than usual and discovered an old logging road that wound its way deep into the woods. Tentatively, we walked a few feet down the trail and into the woods. The pungent aroma of a mature forest in fall—decaying leaves, damp earth, onions, mushrooms and rotting wood—greeted us. Fifty feet above us the brilliant reds and yellows of the autumn forest played against the intense blue of an

autumn sky. The silence was awesome.

Quickly, the woods became a central part of our lives. Our bike rides ended there, our hikes began there and whenever we wondered what to do, one of us said, "Let's walk up the road."

At first we followed the logging trail, but soon the forest lured us from that path. Larry, his interest awakened by the countless specimens that sprung spontaneously from sundry places within the forest, used his botanical training to become knowledgeable about mushrooms. For me the woods was an entirely new world and my interests were less directed than his. I delighted in the pale Indian Pipe freshly thrust from the ground, brown leaves and black dirt still clinging to its translucent sides, and laughed at the fat, old porcupine whose flat, black face peered down at us from his solid perch in a swaying tree. I loved the odor of wild leeks on my fingers and the scent of wood freshly chipped from a topless tree by the pileated woodpecker who flew heavily away as we approached. Then one day I held my breath as a raccoon ambled past, seeking a tree to climb. He was quite unaware of my presence. I was startled by his size and impressed by his confident and leisurely attitude. It was the first time I had closely observed a wild animal living naturally, totally unaware of me, and the experience was unforgettable.

We knew the woods in all its seasons and approached it with any mood. The forest offered us silence when we needed silence; laughter when we felt like laughing. It awakened us to countless activities, entertained us for hours; but it soothed us when our lives were too full of activities and entertainment.

We came to need the woods and wished that we could guarantee its continued existence. We talked of buying the land. Although I hesitated to "own" the land, Larry observed that ownership was a means of preservation.

Of course, we both knew that we could never afford 80 acres of mature hardwood so we enjoyed the land each day, thankful that it still welcomed us.

One day when we especially needed cheering, we drove up the road to the land. Preoccupied, we did not notice our surroundings on the way to the land. But when we emerged from the woods an hour later we were ready to look at the world again and, chatting almost happily, we started home. Even then we almost missed it. My husband spotted it first and had to point it out to me. The leaves and woodline seemed to hide it as if purposely from the casual observer. Stunned, we read "FOR SALE 80 ACRES." With a sickening feeling growing inside us, we copied the realtor's name and telephone number and rushed home to call him. Although we were already sure that we could never buy the land, visions of housing developments, clearcut logging operations or simply "No Trespassing" signs compelled us to make the call. We learned that the land was owned by a lumber company that would sell the land but reserve the right to cut the large timber. Twenty minutes later, with little thought about finances, we accepted the terms and bought the land excluding the timber "11 inches in diameter, 12 inches from the ground." Nearly a month later the deed was signed and the abstract delivered into our hands.

I stand sometimes near one of the largest trees which will soon be felled. I cannot embrace it, the trunk is too thick; I cannot see its top branches, the tree is too tall. I feel insignificant standing in the tree's shadow, and I am impressed anew with knowledge that no one can really own the land. Long before men conceived the idea of deeds and abstracts the land supported life and accepted death. Since the first reported purchase of our land in 1857 for $10.00 per acre, the land has lived through countless owners. At times I'm sure it was purchased for profit and used for financial gain, but I'm equally sure that there were owners who loved it as much as we do.

In friendship, the land offers me sustenance, fun, and well-being. But just as I would not demand too much from a friend, I will not impose myself on the land. I am honored to be its trustee for a time, to learn from its ageless experience and someday to pass the responsibility to another person who will appreciate the opportunity as much as I do.

Autumn Leaves

I read my fate in leaves dancing.
    Like those who predict
        ---their
                futures---
From teacups or stars.

I waiver, am airborne and cruising.
    Like falling leaves
        ---a victim,
                a guest---
Of buffeting winds.

Will I whirl through life like leaves
spinning?
    Mindlessly plummet from
        ---task
            to task ---
Toward earth with a jolt.

Can I be content like leaves drifting?
    Never alter direction but head
        ---slowly
            and straight---
Toward one end.

Should I seek new steps like leaves
fluttering?
    Haphazard moves
        ---first left
            then right---
Toward undefined goals.

Must I fear change like leaves floating
upward?
        Prefer
                ---places
                        I've been---
To challenges unknown.

And when I reach earth
        Crumbling
                ---to
                        dust---
Will it matter how I danced?

A Basket Full of Robins

After the long, silent winter, spring is an audible explosion. One night I fall asleep in silence; the next morning I awake to raucous activity. The last of the snow is gone, and the robins are scratching for worms in the front yard. From then until the next fall I know nothing of solitude. The bees escape their hive and buzz in the blossoming trees. Rabbits raise their young in the raspberries, and squirrels stake claim to the towering oaks. Every nook and crannie of my tangled yard throbs with life. The sparrow builds her nest in the shrubs beneath my bedroom window, giving me a "bird's eye view" of her brood, and the phoebe plasters a mud nest above my just-washed windows.

But it is the robin I wait for. She nests in a planter suspended from macrame rope beside my front door. One especially busy fall I neglected to take this planter inside. Before I knew it, winter had come and gone and the planter still swung on its hook by the door.

One sunny spring morning I gathered my gardening tools and the cuttings carefully hoarded over the winter and set off to fill this planter again. But the robin had already done the job for me. A carefully woven nest camouflaged by the blackened vines filled the planter. Inside the nest, one bright blue egg glistened like a pirate's treasure. I abandoned my gardening tools and set up watch beside the front window. The next day another egg appeared and before the week was out, two more eggs filled the nest. Then the robin settled regally on the nest, and I, fearing to disturb her, began sneaking out of my house through the garage like a thief.

After a while, though, she accepted me, and we shared the front porch. As spring settled into summer, I sat on the front step and watched her on the nest. While her mate trilled melodies from a nearby tree, she set the planter swaying. Extending first her neck and then her tail, she "pumped" the planter like a child pumps a swing. Occasionally she dozed and the planter slowed to a stop. Then her black eyes fluttered open and she began pumping the planter again. As afternoon drifted toward evening she rocked in her nest waiting for her brood to hatch.

I couldn't help comparing her to many women I know who race from career to children to housekeeping in a constant, anxious whirl. I wonder who understands fulfillment best.

Even when her brood hatched, their mouths expectantly open, she seemed to find time for herself. One day in particular when the little ones were about a week old, my husband began to worry. "I haven't seen either robin all day," Larry said. "Something must have happened to them. Now what'll we do?"

We did feel a sense of responsibility to those four open mouths. After all, they were our neighbors. Whenever I opened the front door four heads waved on spindly necks in my direction. Larry liked to tap on the planter and watch those four beaks open in unison, hoping for a handout.

So by mid-afternoon when the parent robins had not been spotted, we did the only thing we could. We found a metal can and our shovel and went digging angleworms.

"Now we'll have to stay home this weekend and feed robins," Larry fumed. But I could tell he was secretly pleased.

"Birds pulverize worms before they feed them to their young," I volunteered, vaguely remembering a nature film I had seen a long time ago. "How are we going to mash up these worms?" The thought sent shivers up my spine.

"That's the mother robin's job," Larry said with a

glint in his eye.

"Oh, no," I answered quickly. "Birds have always shared parenting."

But when Larry set the kitchen stool beneath the nest, I grabbed a wiggly worm and climbed onto the stool first. He looked a little disappointed, but I just could not let him have all the fun.

I dangled the worm above the sleeping downy mound. Nothing happened. I lowered the worm closer to their beaks. Still no response. Larry and I exchanged a worried glance. Had they starved, already?

Then Larry tapped the planter slightly and four open beaks shot upward. I dropped the worm down one of those beaks and fished in my can for another worm. Within minutes the brood emptied my can and were shifting themselves comfortably in the nest.

Our job done for a while, we readied our bikes for an evening ride. That's when we saw them. Both robins were hurrying toward our yard. They rested on a wire for a minute looking for all the world like anxious parents returning from a late night out. "They've been away on a holiday together," I said.

Larry shook his head. "Won't they be surprised to find their family fed," he laughed.

As the days passed, our robins' wobbly heads grew steady, and their downy fluff changed to sleek brown flight feathers. During the hot summer afternoons they spread their sturdy wings and eyed the world below them. We joked about their inadequate housing and marveled that they got along so well, cramped as they were in the crowded nest. We tapped the nest whenever we could because we knew before long they would leave us. Then one day as swiftly as the first egg had apeared the robins were gone. Once again my empty planter swayed slowly on its hook by the door and solitude began creeping into my yard.

I was not as busy that fall as I had been other years, but even then I did not take the planter down. I wanted it to be ready when the robins returned in the spring. They should be here any day.

Autumn Adventure

In autumn I share the road with strangers. They come in khaki-colored shirts and clumsy boots to track animals.

"Did you see anything?" I hail one of them as he emerges from the wood. He shakes his head, disgruntled.

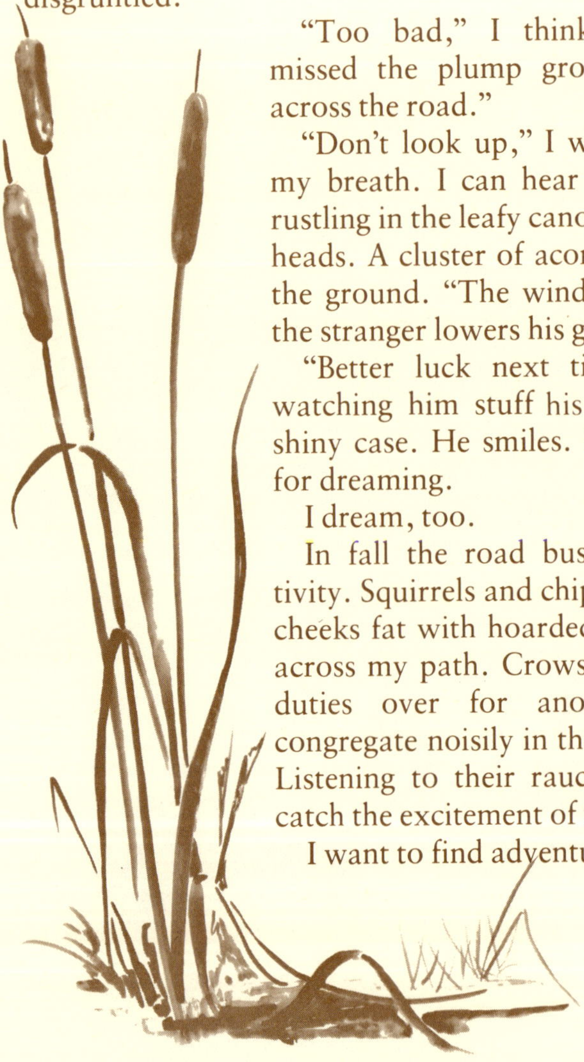

"Too bad," I think, "you just missed the plump grouse strutting across the road."

"Don't look up," I whisper under my breath. I can hear the squirrels rustling in the leafy canopy above our heads. A cluster of acorns flutters to the ground. "The wind," I say, and the stranger lowers his gun.

"Better luck next time," I add, watching him stuff his gun into its shiny case. He smiles. Fall is a time for dreaming.

I dream, too.

In fall the road bustles with activity. Squirrels and chipmunks, their cheeks fat with hoarded nuts, scurry across my path. Crows, their family duties over for another season, congregate noisily in the tallest trees. Listening to their raucous voices, I catch the excitement of the season.

I want to find adventure, too.

Do I hear something rustling in the brush? Expectantly, I set off to investigate.

At the edge of the road, my foot sinks into the soft earth. I look down. My worn sneaker nearly covers an imprint in the mud. Visible around the rubber toe of my tennis shoe are long scratch marks. "Claws?" I think, my heart pounding.

"What would make such a large track?" I ask myself, glancing apprehensively up the road. The loping tracks continue along the shoulder for as far as I can see. "A bear," I whisper, scarcely daring to breath.

I remember the time I saw two bear cubs tumbling in the field just over the hill. They were brawling and batting at each other in the sunlight. When I ran toward them, they vanished, seemingly in mid-air. Later, when I thought of the danger, I was thankful that they had vanished, but I never quite recovered from the disappointment of their disappearance. "Next time," I promised myself, "I'll be more careful."

But now I am frightened. Cubs are cute, but a bear whose track engulfs my own is another matter. I turn my back and head home.

"I've seen a bear," I tell my husband. "Well, his tracks anyway."

"Where?" he says, reaching for his hat.

"On the road," I say, the excitement building. "Come, I'll show you." Together, we set off on the adventure.

Soon the tracks appear. They are large, deep scratch marks outlining one end of a rounding pad. "See," I say, "bear tracks."

He bends to examine them carefully, crouching along the road like a mountainman.

Glancing nervously around me, I stand stiffly over the first track-- waiting.

After what seems a long time, he says softly, "These aren't bear tracks."

"They are," I insist. "See the claws, here," I say pointing. "See the pad," I add, sinking my hand into the print.

"I want to think they are bear tracks as much as you do," he smiles, "but no bear has seven claws."

I count the scratch marks. Seven!

"What about the pad?" I plead.

"Just an impression," he says. "Looks like some kind of farm machinery dragging a part. See how the marks turn out? No bear was ever that pigeon-toed."

I risk a smile then. I'm secretly glad it is not a bear. I've enjoyed the dream more.

By the time we leave the tracks, the sun is high above the road. It has warmed the moist dirt to dusty grains of sand. We spy a grouse dusting himself just ahead of us. Together, we stalk him. Taunting us, he lets us get close before he explodes from his bath and showers us with dust. We blink and laugh.

In autumn, the road hums with adventure.

Biking Country Roads

Biking along country roads is one of my favorite pastimes. I like the peace--- and the excitement. The unmistakable aroma of just-mown hay hovers in the still summer air. The sun warms my face, and the colorful weeds growing in the ditches nod as I drift past. The rhythmic whirring of bike tires on the crushed granite of the country road blends with the steady drone of a distant tractor. Both sounds are welcome in the quiet afternoon. They are reminders that people belong in the country, too. Even the sleek, red doe who steps into my lane does not consider me an intruder when I am bike-born. I coast to within touching distance of her before she leaps into the woods with a farewell flick of her famous tail.

Not all animals are as placid as the deer. A country bicyclist is considered fair game by rambunctious farm dogs. They lurk in ditches and sprint from behind buildings to greet me. Some of these dogs mean to be friendly, but others view the bike's flashing spokes as an invitation to the chase. Predicting the intention of each dog adds excitement to biking country roads.

Since the first dog lunged snarling at me from his hiding place in an overgrown ditch, I have been suspicious of country dogs. I keep a sharp look-out for them and usually execute a "mailman maneuver" when one rushes toward me. Squealing my bike to a halt, I talk soothingly to the dog while I walk the bike past his territory.

Sometimes this works and sometimes it does not. Queenie, a huge black Labrador, is one of the dogs that is wise to my techniques. She knows I do not mean the nice things I say about her. Most dogs stop when I jump from my bike, but Queenie circles the bike slowly. Then she falls in step at my heels. Her thick black hair raises menacingly along the back of her neck as she escorts me to the edge of her territory. When she is satisfied that I am past her land, she returns to her yard. Through the trees I can see her dociley submitting to the pulls and tugs of friendly children.

Sometimes I feel brave and accept the challenge of a defensive dog. Then I try to outrun my pursuer. Occasionally this bravado gets me in trouble. One day in particular was nearly my undoing. As the little mut ran barking across the yard, I thought I could outrun him. When he reached the driveway, I realized I had guessed wrong. This dog was out for blood. Forced to choose between calling his bluff and swerving in front of a speeding truck, I chose to take my chance with the truck. Heedless of the two-ton-van barreling down on me from behind, I pulled into the traffic lane to avoid the two-pound terrier yapping at my heels. Interestingly, I was rescued by an older dog. Nipping at the pup's throat, the other dog sent him scurrying for the yard. I regained the shoulder seconds before the truck rushed past me.

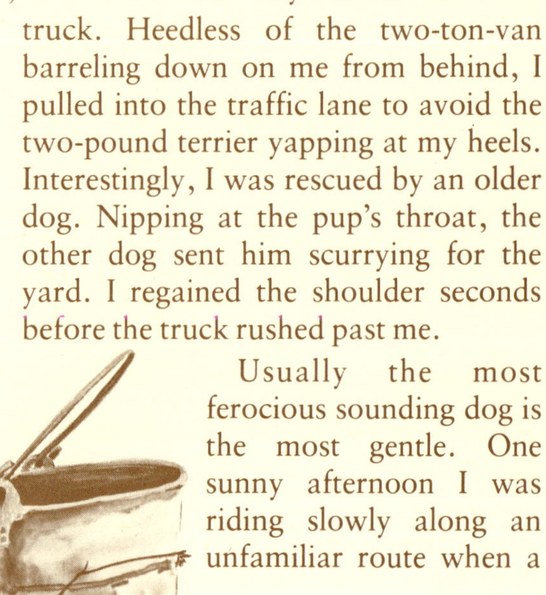

Usually the most ferocious sounding dog is the most gentle. One sunny afternoon I was riding slowly along an unfamiliar route when a

huge farm collie pushed open the kitchen screen door and bolted, barking loudly, directly for me. I leaped from my bike and prepared for battle as the old woman shouted assurances of the dog's good nature from her vantage point on the porch.

When the dog reached me, he stopped and sniffed inquiringly at my heels. I risked a pat on his whitened muzzle. Grateful for the attention, he peered at me with cloudy, near-blind eyes. Then, contented that he had greeted the visitor properly, he limped arthritically back to his rug on the farmhouse porch.

One of my favorite routes is past a yard full of scamps. Two white huskies, three mixed-breed terriers and a spaniel or two line up along the ditch as I ride by. A husky barks once; his twin barks twice. A terrier takes a step forward; the whole ragged line advances. I wave and call as I pedal past. Some of my best friends, these days, are the animals I meet on the biking trail.

I have been challenged, chased and charmed by country dogs, but other thrills also await the country bicyclist. I have been pursued by some surprising assailants. One summer evening I was toiling up a steep hill. The low orange sun silhouetted a healthy herd of beef cattle grazing in a nearby pasture. "Thank goodness cows are fenced in this county," I thought. I was reluctant to try my "mailman maneuver" with 800 pounds of beef on the hoof.

As I pedaled closer to the pasture, the cattle became uncomfortably large. I searched the fenceline for assurance. At first I thought the sun deceived me by obscuring the wire. But finally I admitted that the fence was down and I was approaching twenty loose and curious cows. In panic, I decided to pretend nonchalance. The young stock quit grazing and stared at me as I pedaled determinedly past them. Then one sturdy steer stepped away from the herd. As his stocky legs carried him toward me, his horns grew steadily longer. I kept pedaling. When I was past him, I risked a glance backward. He was standing forlornly in the middle of the road watching me. "I probably should have stopped and patted his nose, too," I thought before I shifted into high gear and disappeared.

Maybe I will--- next time. It is all part of the fun of biking country roads.

My Favorite Neighbor

An abandoned homestead borders on my property, but I do not consider the dilapidated buildings an eyesore nor the gnarled orchard haunted during a full moon. Instead, I welcome the old place as my most interesting nieghbor.

In early spring I come, empty basket swinging, to borrow from my neighbor. Cutting thick, succulent spears from the asparagus bed still flourishing beside the barn, I learn to respect the wisdom of the gardener who established these roots in such a fertile base. Unlike his transient successors, this person planned to spend his lifetime with the land. Beyond the house, a strawberry patch — reverted to the wilds now — yields perfectly rounded berries of a flavorful tartness unique from their hybrid heirs. Adjoining the strawberry patch, a thriving clump of raspberry bushes promises quarts of berries to the patient scavenger.

Vegetables, fruit and nectar for my bees flourish on this land. Walking home across the spacious fields, I feel a thrill akin with those who first settled here, a special independence born of providing for my needs directly from the land.

Pungent cinnamon roses, old-fashioned lilacs and sweet peas gone wild outline the crumbling fieldstone foundation of the farmhouse. More than the orchard or the cleared fields, these blossoms remind me of the people who shared

25

their lives with this farm. Alone now, the land continues to acknowledge the care of its first guardians.

And I, an intruder upon this relationship, absorb a bit of its loveliness, for I have learned many things while visiting my neighbor. With my neighbor's guidance I have learned to listen for the melody of breezes playing upon the great white pine and to watch for patterns in a spider's web. I have also learned to welcome solitude because I realize that loneliness need not be connected with being alone.

Inspired by the example of my venerable neighbor, I have filled the sterile greenery of my perfect lawn with bulbs and shrubs and fruit trees. They grow in twisting patterns, spring up in unexpected places and continuously entice me with their changes.

But they also lend a permanence previously lacking in my hurried existence. As I bury a seedling's spindly roots or toss fine seed against the soil, I bond my life to the land. For my neighbor has taught me to value permanence and has shown me legacies the land extends to those who care.

The Country Ditch

Progress came to our road this spring. Thick, hot tar smothered the sun-rusted granite like a sterile shroud. Voracious machinery gnawed greedily at the matted ditch, uprooting willowy shrubs and mowing waving grasses. Fragile wildflowers were crushed beneath mounds of soggy fill dirt. From our front porch we stared across the vacant land at the shining ribbon of black stretching toward the sun and mourned the loss of our ditch.

There is no hierarchy in the roadside ditch; each plant is beautiful and every one is important. In spring, tawny dandelions are as favored as the rare bloodroot gracing our boundary's boulders. Later, orange hawkweed and creeping vetch combine with white and yellow daisies to form kalaidescopic patterns in the summer breeze. Then the purple thistle's fluffy blooms begin to dry and wild canaries flock noisily to feast upon the seeds. Considered noxious weeds by many, these plants transform the roadside into a spectacular garden.

In the late fall when heavy frosts leave barren yards, the country ditch continues blooming. Wild asters' pastel hues blend with chocolate tones of ripening cattails, and velvety goldenrod blazes with the memory of a summer sun. Even in the winter the ditch retains a special charm. Blustery winds cut silvery shapes from the plow-mounded snow and spiney thistles scatter their seeds in bronze designs across the frozen crust.

The country ditch is an abundant source of food; shameless scavengers, we vie with the jays and starlings for the ditch's booty. In mid-summer elderberry shrubs and cherry trees glisten with their garnet-colored fruit; bushes hang heavy with red and black berries; pungent fragrance of wild mint fills the heavy afternoon air.

The tangled beauty and bountiful harvest of the roadside ditch support countless wild creatures. Butterflies refresh themselves on flowering milkweed, grouse hide beneath the shrubs and bees throb steadily among the blossoms. A ground sparrow fashions her nest from last season's grasses. In passing, a deer nips the alder buds. Snakes and rabbits, raccoons and caterpillars all find a haven in the country ditch.

The ditch is also nature's timepiece; its changing character a record of the seasons. A red-winged blackbird resting in a low-branching willow is a certain sign of spring; milkweed fluff the indicator of approaching winter. But this year our hollow ditch cannot gauge the seasons; the animals have all found other homes, and only cultivated flowers wave in neat rows across our lawn.

Idly, we watch heat mirages forming on the pavement. Our memories form other images as we mourn the loss of our ditch.

Our Land is Logged

Selective logging began on our land this week. Although we had been expecting it, we were startled by the discovery. After purchasing the land a year ago from a lumber company (exclusive of timber rights), we had indulged in a favorite fantasy. We imagined that the loggers forgot about our 80 acres or found cutting the timber financially unattractive. We daydreamed that their three-year contract expired, and we legally acquired the giant maples, oaks and evergreens looming impressively across the land.

Although we realized that such hopes were unrealistic, we were free of the nagging reality of our agreement with the loggers as we walked up the road to our land on the last day of our summer vacation. We expected the land would greet us as it always had—with an awesome sense of peace; instead, we felt tension.

Larry examined a scrape mark on one of the boulders embedded in the road and wondered who had been driving into our land.

We stood for a moment on

the road, listening to the silence; then we started slowly down the old logging trail. The huge trees towered over us, but the land seemed changed. We puzzled over a newly dug drainage ditch. Then we heard the persistent drone of a motor, and we knew they had come for their trees.

As we rounded a bend in the trail, we saw three men in the distance. Dwarfed by massive timber, they seemed almost unreal— our fantasy reversed. A tiny man approached a giant tree. The irritating buzz of his toy saw interrupted the stillness for a few seconds. Then, appearing to caress the giant, he laid his hand against the tree's trunk, and the huge tree wavered. Ripping through the still afternoon, it crashed to the ground; the earth trembled.

The crash of a great tree must be, even for those who hear it daily, an awesome experience. For us, it was a shock that sent us hurrying from the land.

When we returned a few days later, the loggers had left their work for the day; the machines were quiet, but the deceptively sweet smell of fresh sawdust warned us of what lay ahead on the path. Huge fallen trees were everywhere, their green leaves withering at wrong angles to the ground. I brushed the sawdust from a maple stump and counted the rings—68. Curious, I counted the rings in other stumps. One freshly cut tree revealed 120. That fallen elm was almost 100 years old when I was born. The rings spun a tale of prosperity and drought. At times I could hardly fit my finger nail between the rings; at other times the rings were almost a quarter-inch thick. I imagined that tree, increasing steadily in girth for more than a century while we struggled through wars, economic collapse, social unrest and numerous minor upheavals, and I understood clearly for the first time why we achieve peace through wilderness. In a shocked and transient world, trees continue to grow much the same as they have for millions of years. They do not move unaided from the places of their creation, and they can be depended on to lend a solid backrest, provide homes for small animals and change predictably with the seasons. Although I accepted the circumstances of their cutting, I mourned the loss of my wild place.

"The land will restore itself," Larry assured me. Running my hand thoughtfully over the unblemished wood of the ancient elm, I searched for similar optimism. A foot-high seedling sprouted near the great trunk. Two full-sized leaves fluttered on the stick-like stalk. They stretched themselves toward the sky, their leaves turning reddish in the autumn sun. I began to hope for the land.

Larry and I have returned to our land many times since that first week. The loggers continue to cut roads across the woodlot, and we wander the maze, searching for direction. We will not abandon this land even though it has changed. We remember the serenity we once knew here. We continue to savor our commitment to the land.

Under our feet, tiny seedlings flourish in the unexpected sunlight. Stretching their branches in the open air, they point a way for us. The land will restore itself. We intend to help, and through our efforts we expect to know an even greater joy than during that year when we dreamed the giant trees were ours.

The Woodlot

AND STUMPS REMAIN

Sawdust sprays--- a golden blood;
Wood core splinters--- sunbleached bones;
A giant topples with wrenching cries,
The land is logged.

Silence settles--- fragile peace;
Patterns alter--- man's design;
The ravens warn of ruined homes,
And stumps remain.

INTERIM

Fungi thrive--- the cremators;
Exposed earth dries to broken brick;
A roving fox sheds thistle seeds,
While the land waits.

AND HOPE RETURNS

Flowers spread--- a cheerful shield;
Seedlings sprout--- defying death;
As birds appear with rallying cries,
The land revives.

Bustle builds--- a welcome sound;
Charm's restored--- a miracle;
Nature heals machine-scarred earth,
And hope returns.

Spring

Spring came to our road today. Moisture, trapped during the long winter, bubbled to the spongy surface, and the small stream crested, cutting channels into the soft, red clay. "Road Closed" signs appeared where gravel meets the blacktop. For a time, now, the road is mine, alone.

My worn boots leave ragged patterns in the mud. Undisturbed from day to day, these imprints guide me to familiar pleasures. My tracks blend with those of the deer, raccoon and fox, the creatures which share this road with me. We all feel more free in spring when we do not need to watch for cars.

We do watch for holes, however. The spring thaw leaves large openings in the road. These holes begin with the first warm weather. Water rushes into air pockets which have formed beneath the surface of the road. As the road settles, the water is forced to the surface. Clumps of clay break off, drop into the air pockets and leave ever-widening depressions in the gravel.

I like to peer into the larger holes and watch the frothy water bubble to the surface. Some of these openings seem to drop forever. They remind me of the sipapuh of Indian lore. According to the legend, humans originally arrived on earth through holes in the ground. When a person died his soul returned to the other world through a sipapuh.

The sun casts my shadow across the broken road. The water gurgles in the stillness. I think that sometimes I can catch a glimmer of my soul in the depths of a sipapuh. But I am not ready to return to that other world. It is spring on the road, and I am beckoned onward.

The road rises gently out of the shady lowlands to a sunny field becoming green. I surprise a flock of robins clustered on the saturated ground. What special instinct told them to arrive on the very day the first grubs wriggled to the surface? I crane my neck to see above the granite fence which lines the boundaries of this field. After the long winter, robins—those eagerly awaited signs of spring—are worthy of more than a cursory glance.

The granite fence is a welcome sight, too. All winter it has been hidden beneath the plowed and drifted banks of snow. Now its brown rocks glitter warmly, a restful change from the startling glare of frozen snow. But the rugged contours of the granite boulders also cause me to catch a breath. They are a reminder that even under the warm spring sun people struggle with the land.

Beyond the fence a fertile field stretches toward the woodland. I step off the road and follow the fenceline toward the woods. I've often seen the elusive fox skirt this field on his way to hunt, and I follow his route confident that it will lead me to a special find.

Before my eyes have adjusted to the shadowy woods, I stumble near a flock of woodcock. Waiting until the last second, they lift from the ground and that unique twittering associated with their spring skydance fills the air.

Feeling as though I have intruded in a special world, I return to the road. The more familiar cadence of spring frogs greets me. In the gathering waters of the roadside ditches the first optimistic voices call loudly to their fellow nymphs. One footfall silences the medley, but if I stand quietly beside the road, a few tentative voices are soon joined by a hearty chorus. As long as I am still, they happily include me in their comaraderie.

What draws me to this road each spring? Is it the merry exuberance of these secretive frogs? Am I drawn by the pungent aroma of the dark, damp earth? I know that I am lured with the hope of finding the first wildflower.

My brisk footsteps achieve a harmony with the drumming grouse, and still pondering the question, I reach the blacktop. My slippery shoes grate to a halt on the solid pavement. Automatically, I turn my back on an approaching car and retrace my steps along the road.

Above my head a hawk circles like a kite finally freed. Watching him soar, I know what drives me to this road. Here, no strings tug me downward. What I do is unimportant. The silence of a peaceful spirit is the only requirement for acceptance on the road. In its stillness I, too, am free.

"Bees!"

"Your order number please," the voice droned in my ear.

"A-18340," I said.

"What is it?" the voice asked in a disinterested monotone.

"Bees," I answered.

"What!" the voice shrieked.

"Bees," I repeated calmly.

"Bees?" the voice quavered.

For the first time in my long history of telephone shopping, I was sure the voice on the other end of the line was human rather than computer. The frantic girl must have been visualizing swarms of bees escaping their cage and buzzing around her in the store.

But the order was not sent to the store, after all. It was mailed directly to me. (The salesgirl probably arranged it that way.) The postman, however, did not deliver the bees to my house. Instead, he called me. "When can you pick up your bees?" he asked, trying to sound nonchalant.

"Soon," I answered and heard him sigh with relief.

The post office was quieter than I had expected it to be, considering the nature of my order. A few people were peacefully weighing and stamping their packages with the help of a couple of postal clerks. Not wanting to disturb anyone, I stepped up very close to the mailing window.

"I've come for my package," I said, trying to sound natural.

"What is it?" the clerk boomed goodnaturedly.

I cleared my throat, dug my rubber soles into the tile floor and whispered, "Bees."

The rhythmic stamping of the packages stopped. Five pairs of eyes fastened themselves into my back.

"Bees?" the postman whispered increduously. He glanced apprehensively toward the ceiling.

I just nodded, but even the creaking of my neck sounded loud in the stillness of the post office.

"They're in the backroom," the clerk at the next window whispered hoarsely. "In the locker," he added, but he did not show any inclination to get them for me. The three of us exchanged glances. Finally, the clerk at my window accepted his fate. He headed resignedly for the locker.

More quickly than I expected, he returned with a small cage held at arm's length. Thousands of black bodies milled tirelessly against the wire mesh of the cage. They sounded angry, and suddenly I did not want them any more than the salesgirl or the postman or the postal clerk had wanted them. I felt, however, that I needed to get out of the post office quickly, and I knew I should not leave empty handed.

Clutching the handle of the pulsating cage, I walked with what I hoped was confidence past five pairs of glazed eyes and disappeared quickly through the swinging doors. Once in my little car, the bees sounded even angrier, and the drive to the country seemed endless.

I felt better as soon as I set the bees in the acre field I call a yard. With guide book propped open on the ground beside me, I pulled on my beekeeping gloves and set to work. First, I soaked a soft cloth in sugar water and, following the book's directions, rubbed it across the wire mesh. I must admit touching that throbbing cage took a bit of courage. As the syrup dripped onto the bees, the angry buzzing changed to a peaceful humming, and I felt ashamed of myself. The poor little beggars were just hungry.

Hiving the swarm was easy. They were so busy gathering syrup from each other's wings that they did not pay any attention to me as I dumped them rather unceremoniously into the hive. The second they touched the beeswax they settled into their new home.

But the queen worried me. I found her in a little cage suspended from the top of the larger box. Four or five other bees milled around her. "Oh, no," I groaned aloud. I'd read about this. When in distress, bees may attack their queen. Somehow, the bees must have slipped inside the queen's cage, I reasoned, and now they were attacking her. I looked at the sugar coated swarm I had just dumped into the hive. They were already building a comb. What would they do without a queen?

Leaving the queen on the ground and the cover off the hive, I ran for the house to call the neighborhood expert on bees. "There are some bees in the box with my queen," I told him. "What should I do?"

He chuckled. "Those are her attendants," he explained. "You don't expect the queen to feed herself, do you?"

Feeling sheepish for the second time that afternoon, I returned to the field, put the queen and her attendants in the hive and carefully placed the cover over the whole brood. Then I left them alone.

But I couldn't stay away for long. During the next few weeks, I biked around the countryside keeping an eye on my bees. One day I found the entire swarm in the honeysuckle; another time they were busy in the clover field. As summer drifted toward fall, they ranged farther

and I—more confident in my beekeeping role—let them
go.

But each evening they return to their little white box
in my field. Weighted down with pollen and swaying
like drunken elves, they buzz around the landing board
at rush hour awaiting their turns to enter the hive.

Watching them, I am grateful I had the courage to
claim the little beggars when they arrived at the post
office. They are delightful companions to country
living. Summer mornings when I step outside, their
contented buzzing helps start my day, and when I return
in the evening, the aroma of ripening honey welcomes
me home. Lately, I've been thinking about ordering
another swarm. I wonder if the catalogue shopping has
been computerized yet. I guess I know one way to find
out for sure.

The Stowaway

In February, wind whirls against our front door and darkness settles early over our valley. We've skied all of our favorite trails, eaten our fill of roasting chestnuts and begun to draw straws for the "honor" of filling the woodbox. Winter's charm is ebbing and spring seems eons away. Then we recall last winter when we sheltered a stowaway, and one of us tells the story as a ritual reminder that green grass and open water will be ours to enjoy again soon.

This is the story.

One chilly evening we threw a heavy log on the fire and pulled our pillows closer to the blaze. That was the first time we heard it— a hoarse croaking sound from the other end of the room. At first we thought the long winter had muddled our senses. We feared we were imagining the sounds of spring. But we heard it again— the unmistakable rumblings of spring awakening. In our living room it sounded like a bullfrog.

Mystified, we traced the persistent rumblings to the south window. We switched on the yard light and peered outside. The pond was solidly frozen and two feet of crusted snow covered the ground. Spring had not arrived undiscovered. We were imagining things.

"Brrreep," the voice said. We looked at our feet. The sound was coming from our feet. "Brrreep," it said again. We were standing beside a huge potted cactus. A family heirloom passed from generation to generation, it was a special plant, but I could not believe it had started to speak.

"Brrreep," it trilled suddenly, and we dropped to our knees to study the plant more closely. Our heads together, flashlight in hand, we peered into the dark recesses of the plant. The cactus was silent.

"It must have been the house settling," Larry said.

We returned to the fire.

"Brrreep," the voice called.

This time we sat very still, searching our memories for a clue from the distant past. Had we heard the sound before? In the spring, perhaps? On a summer walk? In the garden? On the river? Under a tree?

"A tree frog," Larry said suddenly. "It sounds like a tree frog." And I agreed.

Evidently, the little guy had hidden himself in the woody stems of the old cactus and had been carried inside with the plant in the fall. A stowaway, he had slept peacefully through Thanksgiving and Christmas and was just now beginning to stir, promising spring.

In the days that followed, we discovered that our stowaway awakened when the room was warm. Sun shining in the south window started him gossiping. We stoked our nightly fires high in hopes of hearing his cheerful predictions.

As February gave way to March, the tree frog chirrupped louder and longer in the warm room, and we searched the cactus for a glimpse of him. But he remained hidden. We believed him, anyway. We believed that spring was on its way.

And it did arrive, rather unexpectedly and a little earlier than usual. Coming home late one evening we noticed open water on the pond and a scent of moist earth in the air. In our excitement about these first signs of spring, we forgot the tree frog. But he had not forgotten spring. On this first warm night he had moved unerringly from his hiding place in a far corner of the living room to our front door. He sat in the foyer, glistening green on the white tiles, waiting for us to let him out.

"Brrreep! See, I told you," he said.

"Finally, it's spring," we agreed.

In deference to his superior intuition, we opened the

door wide and stepped aside to let him pass. Our stowaway wavered on the threshold for a moment. Then with a final triumphant "Brrreep" he leaped through the opening and disappeared into the night.

For a few days we heard his familiar calls trilling from the open pond, but soon his voice mingled with other spring sounds and we could no longer distinguish it. Spring melted into summer and the cactus waited on the front porch.

Last fall, when we carried the ancient plant in for the winter, we remembered our stowaway. Now, as February closes in on us, we stoke the fire brighter and listen hopefully for his cheerful voice. Maybe this winter we'll be lucky, again.

TOWN HALL

Voting at the Town Hall

I didn't think about it, really. After all, this was not my first experience as a voter. I just parked my car in front of the school, walked in through the front door and told the first person I saw that I had come to vote.

"Vote?" he mused, leaning on his broom. "In this neck of the woods, we vote at the town hall."

"Town hall," I echoed.

"That's right. Take the first road to your left," he said, following me to the door. "That'll be Green Valley. Follow Green Valley two miles 'til you come to Rocky Ridge. The town hall's one mile north on Rocky Ridge. You can't miss it."

I should have known, I thought ruefully as I eased my car over the ruts in Green Valley Road. In the country everything was different.

In the country I blinked at the brightness of the moon and plugged my ears against the sounds of waking birds at 4am. I spent the first two months of country living fearing to leave my house. If I walked out the back door, I disturbed the phoebe nesting under the eaves. If I opened the front door, the robin flew off her nest in the hanging planter. But the birds raised their broods despite me and as summer slipped into fall, I thought I had adjusted to country living.

Now I had discovered that I did not even know how to vote in the country.

The town hall, I thought again as I turned my car north on Rocky Ridge Road. I was used to voting in neighborhood schools with their neat lawns and spacious hallways. I felt comfortable checking in at the white-clothed table and pulling the lever of a giant gray machine. The organization reassured me. The whispering voices seemed appropriate for the solemnity of the occasion.

Ahead on Rocky Ridge Road, I spied a faded red belfry. Surrounded as it was on three sides by woods, I did almost miss it. As I turned into the gravel parking area, I could not help wondering, "Will voting here be legal?"

I had to put my shoulder to the heavy oak door before it creaked open on rusty hinges. After the quiet of the school, the bustle in the town hall surprised me. A fire crackled in the wood stove, a child played single notes on the old upright piano and laughter rang in the air. A voice beckoned to me, and soon I was standing in front of a long table spelling my name to a man wearing a red plaid shirt.

As I collected my ballot, the coffee perked on a hot plate and talk flowed around me.

   ---Crops coming in. A good season.

   ---The ruts in Green Valley Road. Graded smooth as soon as the last of the corn was in.

   ---Another calf-- a late comer-- born this morning.

   ---Honey. Apples. Blackberries. A banner year.

No hush here, I thought, just a merry bustle of living.

Clutching my paper ballot, I parted the gingham curtains of the peach-colored voting booth and stepped inside. A stubby pencil, its writing end shaved by a pocket knife, dangled from a string above the shelf. I deliberated over my ballot longer than usual. Then as voices rose and fell behind me and the door creaked open and closed, I took hold of the stubby pencil and made a heavy, black **X** in one of the squares. Voices hummed steadily and the door slammed shut. I stared at the **X**.

Unlike my machine-cast votes, this **X** did not disappear with the pull of a lever. It remained on the paper, a challenge to me to be right. As I creased my ballot thoughtfully and returned to the bustle of the main room, I appreciated fully and for the first time the responsibility and privilege of making a decision.

Freedom of choice had always been an important idea to me, but I had never really understood its significance until I stuffed my paper ballot through the slit in the padlocked box and smiled into the sunburned face of the man who guarded it.

Since that first time, I have voted often at the town hall. Each time I feel a special thrill.

"What does one vote matter?" Someone asked me recently.

"Where I vote," I said, "one vote counts."

My neighbors and I may not always agree on the issues, but we value the process. Each time I take hold of another stubby pencil and mark my ballot behind the gingham curtain that X stares back at me challenging me to be right, and I am impressed again with my responsibility and privilege to cast one vote.

47

Country Living

"What will you do in the country?"
Friends asked when we left town.

"We'll manage," Larry assured them,
More eager to leave than explain.
Puzzled silence greeted our packing.
Disbelief answered his claim.

"Won't you miss movies?" they queried.
"Won't you miss concerts and plays?"

"I doubt it," he answered,imagining
The woodcock's dramatic ballet.
"No, never," I said with conviction,
Hearing trumpeting geese serenade.

"What will you do in the country?"
They persisted, dissatisfied.

"We'll ski from our doorstep." we told them.
"We'll skate on the neighbor's pond.
"We'll bike down back roads each evening,
And hike through fields at dawn."

"The shopping," they countered, triumphant.
"You'll miss finding bargains in stores."

"Not me," I laughed, unbelieving.
"I'll scavenge for berries instead."
"We'll ferret out fish in the trout streams,
And hunt for nuts," Larry said.

"You'll miss the excitement," they answered,
"Inspiration from galleries and talks."

"What about autumn?" we questioned.
"What about sunsets and stars?
"We'll find inspiration in Nature.
"Let Nature direct our thoughts."

"The country is lonely," they warned us.
"The silence unnerving and dull."

But we welcomed silence and used it,
Enriching values we'd found.
This kinship and peace we're now sharing
With friends who join us from town.

49

Country People

"I don't know if I would like living in the country," a woman said to me at luncheon. "Country people are different,"

"Yes," I agreed, " country people are different."

Country people accept the fluctuations in their lives as easily as they adapt to the changing seasons.

"Aren't you worried?" I asked my neighbor when the rains had held off for months.

"About what?" he replied.

"About Wisconsin becoming a desert," I answered, staring at the stunted corn yellowing on the hilltop.

"It will rain again," he said, his glance following mine. "Bad times don't last forever."

The next year the rains came, and my neighbor cut an extra crop of hay. A farmer in the next county brought in two crops of corn.

Now, I accept the things I cannot change. I endure the frightening times and enjoy the peaceful times because I have learned from my neighbor that neither good times nor bad times will last forever.

I have also learned to respect time. Country people do not fight the clock. Jobs are tackled as they need doing. Tasks left unfinished at the end of the day are taken up the next day. Country people do not rush to complete their work before 3pm so they can go home. They are home. There are no bells in the country. No whistles signal the time to rest. A friend calls the farmer from his field. His body tells him when to rest.

My day is organized by bells. Stop-and-go lights dictate my responses, but I carry a country attitude to my city job. I work through one task at a time and remember that what I do not finish today will wait until tomorrow.

My work is not a burden now. Following the example

of country people, I have put my job in perspectve. No job is so important to my neighbors that they miss the geese migrating over their fields. No task is so demanding that they fail to see the fox cuffing her kits on the hillside. They can smell the rain coming, and they know the exact hour the swallows above the barn door hatched. They feel the warmth of the sun and the sting of the icy rain, and they enjoy them both. These things are as important to them as the price of oats or the demand for beef.

My neighbors always have time to talk, but I rush past them guiltily. My city job leaves me drained, and I avoid companionship. Even the sweet onions and straight carrots my neighbor offers me from her garden do not tempt me. When I notice the bewilderment on my neighbors' faces, I wish that I could stop to talk. I should remember that friendly chatter can be restful, too.

Yes, country people are different. I have learned a lot from country people. I still have much to learn. Some day I hope to be a country person, too.

About The Author

L. F. Abrams

A confirmed woods wanderer, Kathy has hiked the beaches and backwaters, mountains and meadows of America. But her favorite wanderings are the woodlots and gravel roads of rural Wisconsin—her home and the inspiration for these reflections.

Her special kinship with the land is evident in her writings. She shares this relationship with her favorite fellow wanderers, her husband Larry and their dog Gabriel.

Kathy is a freelance writer and photographer. This is her fifth book

About The Artist

K. S. Abrams

"One walk along the shore gives me hundreds of ideas for paintings," say watercolorist Oberon Leslie. Her strong bond with the countryside is evident in the subjects of her art — old barns, stalwart lighthouses, the rugged shores and gentle valleys of her wanderings.

An award-winning artist, Oberon is noted for her color perception. Her paintings reveal the changing blues of a stormy lake and the rosy hues of an evening sky.

She shows her work in galleries and at art shows throughout the Midwest.